Rocks and Minerals

by William B. Rice

Science Contributor
Sally Ride Science
Science Consultants
Nancy McKeown, Planetary Geologist
William B. Rice, Engineering Geologist

MISSION: SCIENCE

Developed with contributions from Sally Ride Science™

Sally Ride
Science

Sally Ride Science™ is an innovative content company dedicated to fueling young people's interests in science.

Our publications and programs provide opportunities for students and teachers to explore the captivating world of science—from astrobiology to zoology.

We bring science to life and show young people that science is creative, collaborative, fascinating, and fun.

To learn more, visit www.SallyRideScience.com

First hardcover edition published in 2009 by
Compass Point Books
151 Good Counsel Drive
P.O. Box 669
Mankato, MN 56002-0669

Editor: Mari Bolte
Designer: Heidi Thompson
Editorial Contributor: Sue Vander Hook

Art Director: LuAnn Ascheman-Adams
Creative Director: Keith Griffin
Editorial Director: Nick Healy
Managing Editor: Catherine Neitge

 This book was manufactured with paper containing at least 10 percent post-consumer waste.

Library of Congress Cataloging-in-Publication Data
Rice, William B.
 Rocks and minerals / by William B. Rice.
   p. cm. — (Mission: Science)
 Includes index.
 ISBN 978-0-7565-3957-3 (library binding)
 1. Rocks—Juvenile literature. 2. Minerals—Juvenile literature. I. Title. II. Series.
QE432.2.R3285 2008
552—dc22   2008007712

Visit Compass Point Books on the Internet at *www.compasspointbooks.com*
or e-mail your request to *custserv@compasspointbooks.com*

Table of Contents

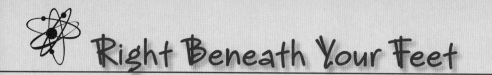

All around you, amazing things are happening. Trees sway to the ever-changing currents of the wind. Clouds drift overhead, dropping rain or blankets of snow. Ocean waves crash forcefully onto sandy beaches. But you may not have noticed the wonderful things happening right beneath your feet. There lies a fascinating world of rocks, minerals, and gemstones.

crust (solid rock)

upper mantle (solid rock)

lower mantle (solid rock)

outer core (liquid metal)

inner core (solid metal)

Many geologists believe that as Earth cooled, the heaviest and most dense materials sank while the lighter materials rose. This is why the core is made of heavy metals while the crust is made of the lightest materials.

Rocks are everywhere, in our backyards and city parks. They're even in our walls, buildings, and roads. And in rocks we find precious jewels for rings and necklaces.

It's a simple thing to walk outside and find a rock. But knowing where that rock came from and how it was formed makes you look at it differently.

Earth is like a giant rock factory. If you dig down far enough, you will find many types of rock being formed under Earth's crust. Heat, water, and pressure are constantly forming an amazing variety of rocks in various shapes, sizes, colors, and textures.

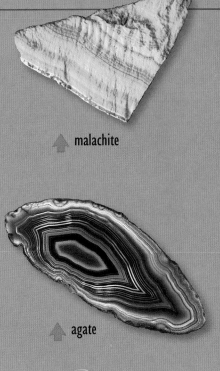
malachite

agate

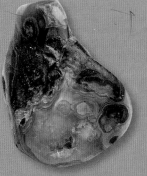
turquoise

amethyst

opal

▲ Geologists regularly measure cracks in Earth's surface at Mount St. Helens, Washington.

Geologists spend their lives studying rocks, minerals, and the structure of Earth. They examine rocks on the surface of Earth and below it. Geologists have discovered that all rocks are made naturally, and they are solid. They have also found that rocks are made of minerals, a naturally occurring substance made of chemical elements.

Geologists have divided rocks into three main categories: igneous, sedimentary, and metamorphic. Although rocks have some things in common, they are also very different. Because rocks are made of various elements and under a variety of conditions, they have their own unique characteristics.

◄ quartz crystal

Rocks sometimes form unique shapes, like the table rock formation in Quebec, Canada.

Studying Earth

There are various types of geologists. They study various aspects of Earth.

- Petrologists study rocks and how they are made.

- Mineralogists study minerals and their properties.

- Hydrogeologists study water in and on Earth.

- Geomorphologists study how natural processes shape the land over time.

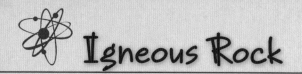

Igneous Rock

Igneous rock is formed from a hot liquid called magma. In fact, the word *igneous* means "made from fire or heat." Magma is found beneath Earth's surface where it is extremely hot. Some types of magma are thin and runny like water or syrup. Others are thick and gooey like honey.

Many igneous rocks form where we cannot see them—under Earth's crust.

They are called plutonic or intrusive rocks. But sometimes magma pushes upward through cracks and holes until it surfaces. It may ooze out slowly, or it may erupt in a scorching spray. Once magma reaches Earth's surface, it is called lava. When lava cools, it forms a type of igneous rock called volcanic or extrusive rock. The word *extrusive* means "forced" or "pushed out."

crack

surface

dikes

rock

sills

magma

magma chamber

Magma rises from below Earth's surface through cracks and fissures. It surfaces in either oozing flows or explosive eruptions.

Eruption!

Sometimes magma gets trapped when it rises toward the surface of Earth. As a result, pressure builds up. When pressure gets too high, magma is forced to the surface. With great force, it erupts, spewing out lava to form a volcano.

In 1991, Mount Pinatubo in the Philippines erupted violently. Gases and dust blew nearly 25 miles (40 kilometers) into the air in an eruption that lasted nine hours. The explosion killed about 800 people and left another 100,000 homeless. It was the second largest volcanic eruption of the 20th century. The largest was Katmai-Novarupta in Alaska in 1912.

Did You Know?

There are at least 1,500 active volcanoes on Earth's surface and another 10,000 beneath the ocean. The oldest known volcano is Mount Etna in Italy— scientists believe it to be around 350,000 years old.

▲ Lava from a volcanic eruption turns into extrusive rock once it cools and hardens.

Intrusive Rock

Inside Earth, hot magma is constantly flowing. Some magma seeps into underground cracks and holes, where it settles and eventually hardens. Magma sometimes gathers in huge underground chambers as wide as 100 miles (160 km). Magma cools and hardens more slowly in these large areas. The magma that hardens underground is called intrusive igneous rock.

The building blocks of all rocks are minerals. And elements are the building blocks of minerals. Various elements can combine to make more than 3,000 kinds of minerals. Oxygen and silicon are the two most common elements in igneous rock. Other elements commonly found in rock minerals are iron, magnesium, calcium, sodium, and potassium.

Extrusive Rock

When magma pushes through Earth's surface, it comes out through openings called volcanoes. Magma contains hot gases that sometimes cause violent eruptions. If magma is low in gas, the magma, now called lava, may flow calmly across the land. It forms gently sloping volcanoes like those in Hawaii.

If magma is high in gas, huge explosions blast lava, gas, and dust high into the air. The flow of lava can reach speeds of 100 miles per hour.

Cooled, hardened lava forms volcanic or extrusive rock. A common example of extrusive rock is basalt, a dark, heavy volcanic rock.

Basalt

The well-known Rosetta Stone is a slab of extrusive igneous rock called dark basalt. It dates back to 196 B.C. in ancient Egypt. The message carved into the stone appeared in two languages (Egyptian and Greek) using three different scripts (hieroglyphic, Greek, and demotic).

Archaeologists later used the Greek carvings to decipher hieroglyphics in Egypt. The stone currently resides in the British Museum in London.

Sedimentary Rock

Sedimentary rock—the second rock category—is all over the planet's surface. It's on sandy beaches, river bottoms, and lakebeds. The formation of sedimentary rock begins with a process called weathering.

Wind, water, snow, and ice are constantly breaking down solid rock into smaller pieces called particles. Extreme heat and cold, as well as chemicals, plant roots, animals, and people, cause particles to break off. Then gravity does its work. It carries particles from the highest to the lowest places on Earth.

Some particles are as large as boulders, while others are as fine as dust. Particles are named according to their size. Wind and water take smaller particles on long journeys, eventually depositing them in lakes or oceans. Large, heavy pieces don't go very far.

1. Fast-moving water picks up rocks and soil.

The amount of sediment a river can carry depends on the speed and volume of the river's flow.

2. The water slows down and deposits some rock and soil.

3. Some sediment gets all the way to the ocean.

Fun with Fossils

Have you ever seen a rock that looks like a bone or has the print of a plant on it? These rocks are called fossils. Fossils form when sediment quickly covers dead plants and animals. Over millions of years, the remains turn into rock.

Fossils tell us a lot about what kinds of creatures once lived on Earth. We learn about fascinating animals such as dinosaurs and saber-toothed cats by examining their fossils.

But water can carry sand or silt a long way.

These bits and pieces of deposited broken rock are called sediment. As rock particles are deposited over and over, layers of sediment build up. Most sediment settles at the bottom of rivers, lakes, and oceans.

Sediments

Size	Particle name
house, car	boulder
football, apple	cobble
peanut, marshmallow	pebble
grains of sugar, grains of salt	sand
flour or dust	silt or clay

Over time, hundreds and even thousands of feet of sediment pile up in layers. Sediment is very heavy. The upper layers put huge amounts of pressure on the lower layers. Eventually, particles in the lower layers are pressed and squeezed together so tightly that they form solid rock. This is called sedimentary rock.

When sedimentary rock gets pushed down far enough, Earth's intense heat and strong pressure melt it. Then it becomes hot magma, which will eventually cool and harden into intrusive or extrusive igneous rock. Isn't that where we began? Yes, rocks have a cycle. From magma to igneous rock; from igneous rock to sedimentary rock; and from sedimentary rock back to magma—this is called the rock cycle.

The Grand Canyon, one of the most impressive examples of erosion
▼ in the world, was carved through many layers of sedimentary rock.

Skeleton Rocks

One kind of sedimentary rock is made of dead animal parts, not rock particles. Shells and skeletons of ocean creatures such as fish, clams, and lobsters can eventually turn into rocks.

Some creatures that form rocks are so tiny that they can only be seen with a microscope. When they die, their bodies drop to the bottom of the ocean. There they pile up in layers, just like sedimentary rock. Over thousands or millions of years, pressure squeezes them into rock called limestone.

Sedimentary Rocks

Made of	Name
pebbles and cobbles	conglomerate
sand	sandstone
silt and clay	shale

Layers of sedimentary rock are easily seen ➡ in a canyon, which was formed by wind and water erosion.

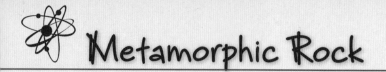

Metamorphic Rock

The third main type of rock is actually recycled rock. It is called metamorphic, meaning "to change form." Metamorphic rocks begin as igneous or sedimentary rocks and then "morph," or change. What causes rocks to change?

Rocks are always changing. They look like they will last forever, but rocks are unstable. Heat and pressure can cause rocks to transform into a new kind of rock. Some rocks change when temperatures rise to just above 392 degrees Fahrenheit (200 degrees Celsius). This is called low-grade metamorphosis. Shale changes into slate in this process.

As temperatures and pressure increase, slate changes into phyllite, then schist, and finally gneiss. This happens during intermediate-grade metamorphosis. Under very high pressure and temperatures that rise to 1,472 F (800 C) and above, gneiss partially melts into migmatite. If migmatite melts completely, it becomes magma. And then the rock cycle begins again.

← Quartzite is a very strong metamorphic stone, but builders usually prefer to use granite, which is more beautiful.

Through heat and pressure, granite turns into gneiss, a metamorphic rock.

Rocks to Write On!

Long ago school children didn't always do their schoolwork on paper. Instead, they wrote on small chalkboards made of slate—a metamorphic rock that can easily be split into layers. Slate makes good writing material because it is smooth, flat, and dark in color—perfect for chalk, which is also a kind of rock.

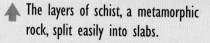

The layers of schist, a metamorphic rock, split easily into slabs.

What would the world be like without rocks? Rocks are not just under your feet. They are everywhere you look. We use rocks to make walls, buildings, roads, jewelry, sculptures, and more.

Igneous rocks have seemingly endless uses. They are used for countertops, floor tiles, landscaping, and construction. They help make steel and insulation. You might find pumice, an igneous rock, in your kitchen sink cleanser or in sandpaper. Granite, rhyolite, basalt, and other rocks are crushed into gravel and used under concrete roads or in concrete itself. Granite is also used for buildings and monuments. The heads of four presidents were carved into a large granite cliff at Mount Rushmore in South Dakota.

A popular sedimentary rock is limestone. It is used for outer walls of buildings, cement, brick mortar, and glass. Gypsum is used in drywall, the material used for building indoor walls.

Metamorphic rocks are also useful. Marble is used for flooring, walls, countertops, statues, and monuments. Slate is used for walkways and roofs, while colorful gneiss makes beautiful outer walls on buildings.

Rocks also hold information about the past. Fossils tell us what kinds of animals and

Marble

Marble is a metamorphic rock formed from limestone. Thin lines and swirls run through the stone, making beautiful patterns. Because of its natural beauty, marble is often used in lavish architecture and ornate buildings. The purest marble is usually white and does not have lines and swirls. This kind of marble has been used to create artistic sculptures.

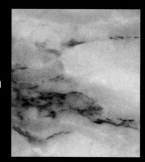

A diamond in its natural state.

A diamond has been cut so it sparkles and can be sold as a jewel.

plants have lived on Earth. They give us clues about what Earth was like long ago. Rocks also provide hints about what Earth might be like in the future.

Rocks are also important because of what is inside of them. They are a treasure chest of rich minerals, crystals, and gemstones.

Marble, limestone, sandstone, and granite are popular choices for building materials.

Vietnam exported more than 35 million tons (32 million metric tons) of coal to more than 30 countries in 2007.

Rocks That Burn

Some rocks produce heat and energy when they are burned. Coal is one of those rocks. It is a hard black rock that can be classified as either sedimentary or metamorphic.

Coal forms underground from dead plants that have been buried for many years. When people discovered that coal burns, they began using it to heat their homes and businesses. Coal is still used today to make electricity and heat buildings. People and machines remove coal from the earth by digging for it in mines.

21

Minerals and Gemstones

Minerals are what make up rocks. Igneous rocks are made of at least two minerals. In pieces of granite, you can see the shiny mineral specks of amphibole, feldspar, mica, and quartz. You probably see some common minerals every day. Pencil lead is made of a mineral called graphite. Most likely, you have seen the mineral halite on your potato chips or in your saltshaker. When salty water evaporates, halite is left behind. In halite's natural form, the soft, cube-shaped crystals are called rock salt.

We don't see minerals such as gold and diamonds as often because they are rare. That is why they cost so much.

Minerals are made up of chemical elements, nature's most basic substances. An element has only one kind of atom. Minerals are a combination of elements.

For example, the elements oxygen and silicon combine to form silica, a mineral commonly called quartz.

Minerals are always solid, but they are different from other solids because of the way their atoms are organized. The atoms of a mineral are arranged in a pattern that repeats itself over and over. This unique arrangement forms a crystal, a three-dimensional structure. Each mineral usually produces the same kind of crystal.

Crystals come in a variety of shapes and sizes. Some are cube-shaped, and others look like pyramids. Some crystals have six or eight sides. Others have 14 or even 18 sides.

Quartz, one of the most common minerals on Earth, is either white or colorless in its purest form.

Hollow, sphere-shaped rocks that contain crystals are called geodes.

White agate is a semiprecious stone used for jewelry and other decoration.

Testing for Hardness

In 1812, scientist Friedrich Mohs created a way to rate the hardness of a mineral based on a scratch test. On the Mohs scale, as it is called, the softest mineral, talc, has a hardness level of 1 because every other mineral can scratch it. In the middle of the Mohs scale is apatite, a rare mineral that can be cut as a gemstone and is used for jewelry. Minerals with a hardness level more than 6.5 can scratch glass. But there is one mineral—the diamond—that no other mineral can scratch. Diamonds have the highest rating—a perfect 10—on the Mohs scale.

Crystals also come in dazzling colors—red, green, pink, blue, purple, and more. Some crystals are clear, and some are white or black. Each mineral also has its own level of hardness. Talc is the softest mineral, and diamonds are the hardest.

Mohs Hardness Scale

1.	Talc
2.	Gypsum
3.	Calcite
4.	Fluorite
5.	Apatite
6.	Orthoclase feldspar
7.	Quartz
8.	Topaz
9.	Corundum
10.	Diamond

Did You Know?

Only a diamond can scratch another diamond. However, scratching two diamonds against each other will damage both diamonds.

Quartz is one of the most common minerals on Earth beause it is formed from the two most abundant elements in Earth's crust—oxygen and silicon. When underground magma cools down, quartz forms as six-sided crystals. Many types of metamorphic, igneous, and sedimentary rock contain at least a small amount of quartz.

Quartz is a 7 on the Mohs Hardness Scale. Because it is so hard, quartz is a very useful mineral. It is used in concrete, glass, sandpaper, electronic products, and jewelry. Rock crystal, a type of quartz, is used for lenses in microscopes and telescopes. Since quartz can withstand high temperatures, it is used to make glass baking dishes.

Many early civilizations believed rock crystal quartz was permanently frozen ice.

Galena, another common mineral, forms in underground areas where hot water flows through cracks in rocks. Galena usually develops into shiny, silver, cube-shaped crystals that contain lead and silver. Unlike quartz, it is rather soft.

Galena's cubelike shape makes it easy for geologists to identify.

Rock Windows

Glass was once very expensive and hard to get. People used large sheets of the mineral mica for "glass" for their windows.

Mica forms into layered crystals similar to the pages of a book. The layers are thin, flexible, and transparent. Even though mica is not completely clear, the sun does shine through it. Mica was a useful material for windows, letting in sunshine and keeping out rainy weather and bugs.

Olivine is a mixture of magnesium or iron, silicon, and oxygen. Nearly as hard as quartz, it is found mainly in dark, igneous rock such as basalt. This yellow-green, dark green, or brown mineral forms into many-sided crystals. Some types of olivine are used as gemstones.

The value of a gemstone depends on its color, hardness, and sparkle. The most expensive diamonds are clear. But diamonds with impurities can be pink, purple, blue, green, brown, or black.

Gemstones used in jewelry have to be at least 7 on the Mohs Hardness Scale. And they have to sparkle. A gemstone's sparkle is measured by how much a ray of light bends when it passes through the gem. The more the ray bends, the better the gemstone.

Did You Know?

There are more than 4,000 known minerals on Earth. Out of these, 70 can be classified as gemstones. Of these 70, only around 20 are commonly encountered in nature.

Synthetic gems are becoming more popular because of their lower price and greater variety. These lab-created gems are made by simulating the heat and pressure naturally occuring deep within Earth. Some popular synthetic gems are emeralds, rubies, sapphires, and diamonds.

Gemstones

Beautiful gemstones are used for rings, necklaces, bracelets, and other fine jewelry. They are minerals that are hard enough to be cut and polished. What is your favorite gemstone? Some people like emeralds, the transparent, deep green stone from a mineral called beryl. Other people prefer the deep red ruby, and some like the rich blue color of the sapphire. Rubies and sapphires are the same mineral, corundum, which comes in different colors.

Twelve gemstones are designated as birthstones for each month of the year. Some months have more than one birthstone—for example, November claims both topaz and citrine as its birthstones. Sometimes one stone is the "traditional" stone while the other is the "modern" one, and sometimes more expensive gems are replaced with less expensive and more affordable stones.

Birth Month	Traditional Gemstone
January	garnet
February	amethyst
March	aquamarine
April	diamond
May	emerald
June	pearl
July	ruby
August	peridot
September	sapphire
October	opal
November	topaz
December	turquoise

Minerals are everywhere. They are an important part of our lives. They are in buildings, windows, and televisions. Others are used to make computers, telephones, and cars. Minerals can be found in concrete and steel. And they are in the jewelry we wear. Minerals make up countless items we use every day.

Minerals help geologists identify rocks. Engineers rely on the minerals that are in rocks to determine the best building materials to use.

Even the human body needs minerals to survive and stay healthy. Iron strengthens the blood, while calcium fortifies our bones. Our bodies get many important minerals from the foods we eat and the vitamins we take.

Rocks are not just something we walk on. Earth's giant rock factory provides much more. Rocks give us important materials for our everyday lives. Rocks also provide information about our planet's history and bring beauty and art to our world.

Coins are made from metals found in a variety of minerals such as gold, silver, nickel, steel, zinc, and copper.

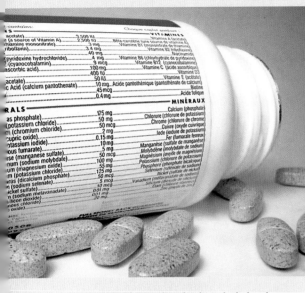

A daily supply of minerals helps keep the body healthy. However, overdosing on certain minerals, like zinc, calcium, copper, or iron, can lead to increased health risks.

Some minerals precipitate, or separate, out of hot springs.

Water Deposits

Minerals are also found in water. You can see them by putting water in a kitchen pan and letting it evaporate or boil away. The white substances left behind are called water deposits, and are an accumulation of minerals. In fact, you can get many of the minerals your body needs just by drinking water.

Have you ever noticed that sometimes water tastes different from other times? This is because naturally occuring minerals in the ground can affect the flavor.

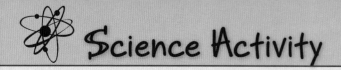
You can learn a great deal about rocks just by looking at them. Follow these steps to see what you can learn.

Materials

- five rocks
- water
- magnifying glass
- notebook
- pen or pencil

Procedure

1. Find five kinds of rocks outside in nature. It is important that they be different. Look around in a variety of places. In your notebook, record where you found each rock.

2. Wash each rock in water, one at a time. When a rock is wet, look at it and observe all the details. You may need a magnifying glass to help you see the tiny features of the rock. What do you see? Record your observations. Here are some things to notice in particular:

   - color or colors
   - presence of crystals
   - size and shape of crystals or particles
   - shininess of crystals or particles
   - amount of one kind of crystal or particle compared to others

3 When the rocks are dry, look at them again, one at a time. Pay attention to the details. What do you see? How does each rock look different when it is dry? Record your observations using the list you used when the rocks were wet.

4 Now make some general observations. Where did you find each rock? What does its location tell you about the rock? Did you find it in a river or stream? Was it on a mountain or in a valley? Was it in a field, by a lake, or at the ocean? Was there anything important in the area where you found the rock? What was nearby that might have affected the rock?

Conclusion

Geologists ask themselves many questions when studying Earth and rocks. To learn about and identify rocks, you'll want to ask lots of questions like the ones listed above. If you want to study rocks even further, you can also test them for hardness or conduct chemical testing. You will need special tools and a lab for these sorts of tests. With the right tools and the right teacher, you can learn many things about the world of rocks and minerals.

Florence Bascom (1862–1945)
American geologist and one of the first female geologists; studied mountains and how they are formed

Winifred Goldring (1888–1971)
American geologist who studied fossils; wrote *The Handbook of Paleontology for Beginners and Amateurs*

James Hutton (1726–1797)
Scottish farmer who is considered the founder of modern geology; he was the first to propose the idea that all geologic features can be explained by rocks from the past; his book, *The Theory of the Earth*, became the basis for modern geology

Charles Lyell (1797–1875)
Scottish geologist who wrote *Principles of Geology*, one of the most influential works on geology; held that fossils were the best guides to describe geologic rock layers; suggested that Earth was millions of years old

Friedrich Mohs (1773–1839)
German scientist who was the first to classify minerals based on hardness; the scale is referred to as the Mohs Scale of Hardness

William Smith (1769–1839)
British surveyor and geologist who wrote the first book used to identify rock layers based on fossils within the rocks; built canal system in England to transport coal to the cities

Nicolas Steno (1638–1686)
Danish geologist credited with identifying the origin of many common fossils

Joann Stock (1959–   )
American professor of geology and geophysics; studies earthquakes that occur on the ocean floor

Alfred Wegener (1880–1930)
German geologist who suggested the idea of the continental drift, that the coastlines of several continents fit roughly together into a supercontinent; paved the way for the theory of plate tectonics

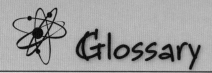

Glossary

basalt—hard, dark rock made from cooled lava

chemical element—substance made of one type of atom

crystal—minerals with an orderly arrangement of atoms

deposition—geological process whereby natural materials are deposited or set down

erosion—wearing away of rock or soil by wind, water, or ice

erupt—to burst or ooze onto Earth's surface

extrusive rock—rock made from magma that erupts from volcanoes and cools rapidly; also called volcanic rock

fossil—remains of an ancient plant or animal that have hardened into rock; also the preserved tracks or outline of an ancient organism

galena—gray mineral that often contains lead

garnet—hard, dark-red mineral that is often used in jewelry

gemstone—crystalline mineral that can be cut and polished for jewelry

geode—hollow, sphere-shaped rock filled with crystals

geologist—scientist who studies how Earth formed and how it changes by examining soil, rocks, rivers, and other landforms

granite—igneous rock with visible crystals; generally composed of feldspar, mica, and quartz

gypsum—sedimentary rock containing the mineral calcium sulphate

halite—sedimentary rock containing sodium chloride; also called rock salt

hardness—relative resistance of a mineral to scratching, as measured by the Mohs Scale

igneous rock—rock formed when magma cools and hardens

intrusive rock—rock made from magma that slowly cooled underground; also called plutonic rock

lava—magma that comes out of a volcano

limestone—sedimentary rock made mainly of the mineral calcite

magma—hot, molten rock beneath Earth's crust

marble—common metamorphic rock often used in construction and for carving statues

metamorphic—changed by heat, pressure, and chemically active gases

mica—natural, glasslike substance that breaks easily into thin layers and is not damaged by heat

minerals—nonliving solids made of chemical elements

Mohs Scale—scale for classifying minerals based on hardness, determined by the ability of harder minerals to scratch softer ones

olivine—mineral consisting of magnesium or iron silicate; a source of magnesium

particle—small piece of matter

quartz—very common, hard, glossy mineral consisting of silicon dioxide in crystal form

rock—the dry, solid part of Earth's surface, or any large piece that sticks up out of the ground or the sea

sediment—small particles of weathered rock

sedimentary rock—rock formed from the hardening of sediment layers

shale—sedimentary rock made from particles of clay pressed tightly together

slate—fine-grained metamorphic rock that splits into thin, smooth-surfaced layers

strata—layers of sedimentary rock

tectonic plates—gigantic slabs of Earth's crust that move around on magma

volcano—vent in Earth's crust from which lava pours; mountains formed from the buildup of lava

water deposits—white substance made of minerals that are left after water boils away or evaporates

weathering—breaking down of solid rock into smaller and smaller pieces by wind, water, glaciers, or plant roots

347 B.C.	Pythias marries Aristotle; together they study Earth
276 B.C.	Eratosthenes is born; later calculates the circumference of Earth
1086 A.D.	Shen Kua's *Dream Pool Essays* describe the principles of erosion, uplift, and sedimentation—the foundations of earth science
1546	Georgius Agricola introduces the word *fossil*
1638	Nicolas Steno is born; later discovers a fossil of a shark's tooth and studies rock strata
1743	Christopher Packe makes a geological map of the southeast portion of England
1760	John Michell proposes that earthquakes are caused by one rock layer rubbing against another
1774	Abraham Werner introduces a classification of minerals
1785	James Hutton presents his paper, "The Theory of the Earth," in which he suggests that Earth is old
1799	William Smith creates the first large-scale geological map of England and Wales; later wins the first Wollaston Medal for achievement in geology; Mary Anning is born; later recognized for her fossil collection
1809	William Maclure completes the first geological survey of the eastern United States; called the "William Smith of America"
1812	Friedrich Mohs creates the Mohs Scale to measure the hardness of minerals

1830	Charles Lyell publishes his book, *Principles of Geology*, in which he states that the world is several hundred million years old
1862	Florence Bascom is born; first woman to receive a doctoral degree from Johns Hopkins University
1888	Winifred Goldring is born; becomes first female state paleontologist in 1939
1907	Bertram Boltwood uses uranium to determine the age of rocks
1911	Arthur Holmes uses radioactivity to date rocks and states that Earth is 3 million years old
1912	Alfred Wegener puts forward the continental drift theory, that the continents were once joined together as a single land mass
1925	A German expedition discovers the Mid-Atlantic Ridge, a mountainlike ridge through the Atlantic and Arctic Oceans resulting from the separation of tectonic plates
1935	Charles Richter develops a scale to measure the intensity of earthquakes; it is called the Richter Scale
1953	Bruce Heezen maps the Mid-Atlantic Ridge
1990	Oldest portion of the Pacific plate is found
2007	Geologist Vicki Hansen hypothesizes that early meteorites created the first rifts in Earth's crust, which in turn jump-started the movement of plate tectonics
2008	Scientists discover that hydrocarbons, an essential building block of life, are naturally generated on the ocean's floor

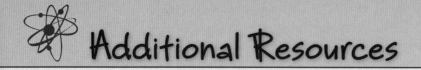

Additional Resources

Dussling, Jennifer A. *Looking at Rocks*. New York: Grosset & Dunlap, 2001.

Hynes, Margaret. *Rocks & Fossils*. Boston: Kingfisher, 2006.

Ricciuti, Edward. *Rocks and Minerals*. New York: Scholastic, 2002.

Stille, Darlene. *Igneous Rocks: From Fire to Stone*. Minneapolis: Compass Point Books, 2008.

Stille, Darlene. *Metamorphic Rocks: Recycled Rock*. Minneapolis: Compass Point Books, 2008.

Stille, Darlene. *Sedimentary Rocks: A Record of Earth's History*. Minneapolis: Compass Point Books, 2008.

On the Web

For more information on this topic, use FactHound.

1. Go to *www.facthound.com*

2. Type in this book ID: 0756539579

3. Click on the *Fetch It* button.

FactHound will find the best Web sites for you.

Index

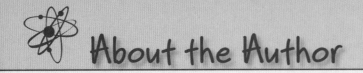

William B. Rice

William Rice grew up in Pomona, California, and graduated from Idaho State University with a degree in geology. For 18 years, he has worked at a California state agency that strives to protect the quality of surface and ground water resources. He has overseen the evaluation and cleanup of pollution in ground water and water in rivers, lakes, and streams. Protecting and preserving the environment is important to him. He is married with two children and lives in Southern California.

Image Credits

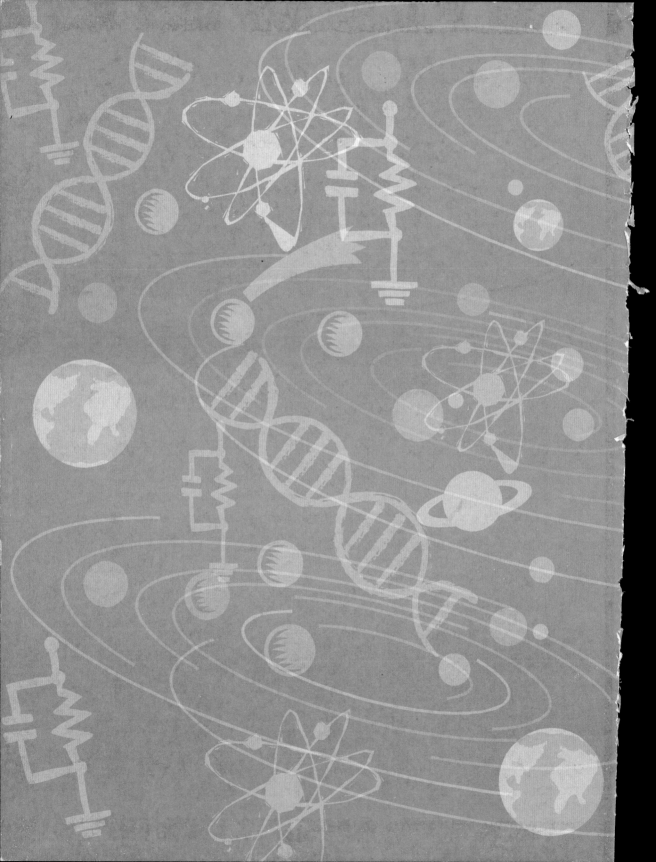